D0256235

IT'S EASY BEING GREEN

IT'S EASY BEING GREEN
A Handbook for Earth-Friendly Living

Crissy Trask

Illustrations by Mike Clelland

Gibbs Smith, Publisher
Salt Lake City

First Edition
10 09 08 07 06 9 8 7 6

Published by
Gibbs Smith, Publisher
P.O. Box 667
Layton, Utah 84041

Orders: 1.800.748.5439
www.gibbs-smith.com

Designed by Martin Yeeles
Printed and bound in Canada

Library of Congress Cataloging-in-Publication Data

Trask, Crissy.
  It's easy being green : a handbook for earth-friendly living / Crissy
Trask ; illustrations by Mike Clelland.— 1st ed.
      p. cm.
  Includes bibliographical references.
  ISBN 1-58685-772-X
1. Environmental protection—Citizen participation.
2. Environmentalism. 3. Organic living. I. Title.

TD171.7.T73 2006
333.72—dc22

2005027473

For my husband.

CONTENTS

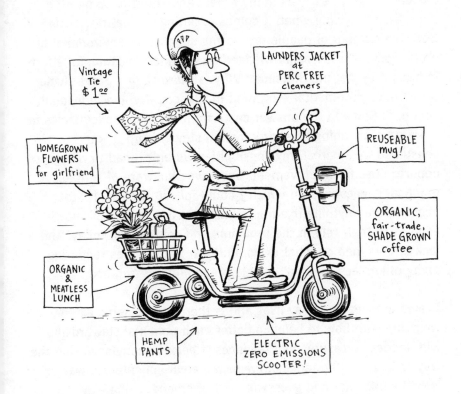

INTRODUCTION

Many Americans agree with the goals of the environmental movement. Yet, nearly as many Americans admit to doing little more than recycling when it comes to acting on that disposition. Both the number of people expressing support for environmental protection and their acknowledged lack of more meaningful efforts to back it up got me thinking, "Why is there such a great divide between environmental sentiment in this country and individual actions?" Clues to the answer came from my own inadequacies in the area of meaningful environmental stewardship. I was consumed by a career, my sensibilities weren't tuned to recognize opportunities for improvement, and I was unaware of simple, practical suggestions on which I could follow through. If other people were anything like me, a busy lifestyle, a lack of knowledge as to their role in the problems and solutions of today, and a lack of guidance on what to do and how to do it was rendering many other "eco-minded" people predominantly "un-eco."

Everyone is leading busy lives and is therefore, to some extent, wrestling with how to balance better environmental stewardship with modern pressures and reliances. I became convinced that the way to increase the ranks of *practicing* environmentalists was to take the difficulty and guesswork out of greener living—by adjusting expectations, stressing learning as a motivator and enabler, and above all else, providing constructive tips and resources to prepare the eco-inclined for action on terms they could live with. It made sense that if busy people were going to start doing more, they would need a lot more help.

It's Easy Being Green is a remedy for that which has held back more people from making better choices for the environment: inadequate information, the uncertainty of what to do, the apprehension of activism and lagging motivation. This is a book that supplies what the busy person needs to start making changes today. It cultivates an appreciation for the cause-and-effect relationship between actions and real environmental harm; it prescribes practical and actionable solutions that can be carried out without aggravation; it promotes the gradual integration of new behaviors and solutions in order to retain what is learned and sustain improvements; and it includes Internet resources and tools for the distinct help they can provide with great ease and efficiency.

This book provides the conscientious reader with a new or renewed consciousness to recognize the need and occasions for improvements and concurrently presents a plan, tips and resources that busy people can use to follow through on good intentions. If you haven't invested in substantially greener behaviors, consumerism and politics because you didn't know how or thought it was difficult, help is here: *It's Easy Being Green* is a handbook for all those who aspire do more to protect the environment but want it to be simpler.

CHAPTER 1:
GREEN LIVING MYTHS

Present-day trends include disappearing wilderness and farmland, irresponsible consumerism, the poisoning of our waterways, species decline and an arguably corrupt political system that panders to exploitative special interests. Turning the tide on such destructive and discouraging trends requires all of us to learn to appreciate how our own behaviors contribute to these problems and to recognize opportunities and occasions to act in ways that can reverse these trends or at least diminish their impacts.

Adopting better habits and ways of doing things doesn't require riches, inordinate discretionary time or overhauling your life, but these could be a few of the misperceptions that inhibit more Americans from acting on their predilection for a healthy environment. Disabusing some common myths about greener living may help remove remaining apprehensions about committing to and acting on some meaningful changes that will enrich your life and make a difference to our world. Consider the following myths and the truths behind them.

> "The problems that exist in the world today cannot be solved by the level of thinking that created them." **Albert Einstein**

EARTH-FRIENDLY LIVING IS A VIRTUE, NOT AN OBLIGATION.

It is now common knowledge that the biggest problems facing our global environment stem from human activities. If these problems are to be arrested or remedied, who else but humans will turn the tide? It's not virtue that produces results when taking on many of life's challenges head on. It's only with a sense of purpose and responsibility that great things are achieved. Be it career, family or the environment, as a society, and personally, we are obligated to put forth a certain amount of effort to succeed in achieving what we need to live and protecting what has value. Our obligation to at least try to pay our own way in life, raise our children into healthy, productive and ethical members of society, and lighten our impact on the earth, among other things, is real.

IT WILL BE TOO DIFFICULT AND DISRUPTIVE TO CHANGE MY HABITS.

There may be a period of adjustment as you embark on turning bad habits into better ones, but difficult and disruptive hardly describe the changes prescribed in this book. Especially when you consider that changing habits and situations can occur a little at a time and over the course of many weeks, making corrections manageable. Changes do not have to be immediately broad and uncompromising. You can start by making small and simple improvements and build on them.

After doing something a certain way long enough, it becomes automatic, but just because something has become automatic doesn't mean that replacing it will be difficult. Forming new eco-friendly behaviors is simply a process of time, repetition and growth. Even in areas where you may have deep-rooted habits, rethinking the full experience and implications of those habits can reveal how unsuitable they really are. Take our dependence on the automobile, for example: do we love asphalt landscapes, traffic jams, road rage, brown skylines and filling our tanks at the pump? Much of the driving people do is more of a habit than a convenience, pleasure or necessity. And like all habits we want to break, we need only find a new one to replace it. Reducing how many days we do the driving—and letting a carpool buddy or public transit worker pick up the slack—reduces stress, accidents and traffic as well as expenses for gas, insurance, tickets, parking and vehicle maintenance. Giving up your car two to three days a week when transportation alternatives exist isn't a hardship, it's just an adjustment.

EARTH-FRIENDLY PRODUCTS ARE HARD TO FIND AND EXPENSIVE.

The natural and sustainable products industry is estimated to be a $230 billion industry nationally, growing by 20 to 30 percent annually. There are thought to be approximately 13,000 retailers devoted to selling environmentally preferable products,[1] and conventional retailers, not wanting to lose traditional customers who are "going green," have begun integrating safer, natural and sustainable alternatives into their assortment. (The easiest way to find out what conventional retailers are offering in the way of lower-impact products is to go to their Web site and search for keywords like "recycled" or "organic." Any and all products with descriptions containing your keywords will be revealed to you.) And there are countless more green businesses operating exclusively on the Web. Finding green products is easier than ever and getting easier all the time.

As far as price, many earth-friendly products are as economical, or more so, as their conventional counterparts because they often utilize recycled or reclaimed materials, require less processing and output less waste than would otherwise have to be managed. There are also many examples of deferred savings after an initially higher expenditure—as in the case of energy-efficient products that reduce energy costs in the long run.

Some earth-friendly alternatives do cost a bit more than their conventional equivalent at the present time, but a well-rounded green buying strategy that includes seeking out energy-efficient, enduring and used products—all of which save you money—can bring down your total average expenditures.

IF I TURN MY BACK ON CONVENTIONAL BUSINESSES, THE ECONOMY WILL SUFFER.

In the expanded marketplace of wisdom and emerging alternatives, "conventional" applies to companies, practices and products that persist in a standard or traditional use of disfavored practices and materials when environmentally preferable ones are both technologically and financially viable. Now that we're clear on the definition of "conventional," let's explore the fallacies in the belief that deviating from the status quo in purchasing will cause the nation's economy great harm.

A shift in consumer loyalties is typical in a market economy. It is a fundamental precept for a strong market economy and a catalyst for economic prosperity. Demand for new and different products and technologies gives rise to new markets—spawning innovation, competition, investment, market growth and jobs. For example, rejecting fuel-inefficient vehicles, the majority of a typical automaker's product assortment, in favor of an electric/gasoline hybrid car will only result in the decline of traditional automakers if they choose to ignore the emerging trend. Corporations are in business to stay in business, and under good leadership, they will change with consumer demand to stay relevant and competitive. Those companies that won't change will quickly be replaced by businesses that can

meet consumer demand—sustaining a robust and viable economy.

Furthermore, it's absolutely necessary that our consumer choices support less wasteful and harmful products and cleaner, sustainable production of the things we need. Economies are only as sustainable as the ecosystems and resources they rely upon year after year. As the head of the United Nations Environment Programme said, "Ecosystems and the services they provide are financially significant and . . . to degrade and damage them is tantamount to economic suicide." Companies that don't respect this certainty, but have your business anyway, will have no incentive to make modifications. Therefore, turning your back on conventional businesses that you have judged to be unaccountable for their actions and disrespecting to the earth is the most important thing you can do to protect our economic future. There is more on this subject in the next chapter.

"The man who goes alone can start today; but he who travels with another must wait till that other is ready." **Henry David Thoreau**

PEOPLE DISPLAYING "GREEN LIVING" PREFERENCES AND BEHAVIORS CAN LOOK CHEAP AND ECCENTRIC.

To some yes, but only to those that are out of touch with emerging trends and the needs of our society and environment. The manifestations of acute intelligence and enlightenment have always been perceived as a bit eccentric—right? In all seriousness, though, most people know enough to accurately judge displays of thrift and conservation for what they are—and respect them—even if this isn't expressed. Those closest to you will certainly know the origin of, and goodness of, for example, your insistence on reusing items several times that most would discard after one use or your efforts to save grey water for use in the garden. As for anyone who doesn't know you, and doesn't get it, their opinion of you shouldn't matter.

THE FRUGALITY THAT GREENER LIVING REQUIRES MEANS DEPRIVING ME AND MY FAMILY OF COMFORTS OF LIFE AND CONVENIENCES I'VE EARNED.

Reasonable comforts and conveniences needn't be sacrificed when committing to greener living. A scale or quantity you're accustomed to may need to be reduced, but the ingenuity and innovation inherent within a capitalist system like ours, often the target of disdain by environmentalists, has nonetheless produced many products enabling earth-minded people to live the good life if this is important to them. Designer home furnishings, state-of-the-art appliances, a nice car, fine cuisine, exotic vacations—these can all be found in earth-friendly form. Just because you're not currently familiar with resources that can provide all these things and more, doesn't mean they don't exist.

Whatever your pet comforts and conveniences are, there is most likely a substitute that will prove to be equally or more satisfying when all the facts are in. Adopting a greener lifestyle doesn't have to be an exercise in deprivation unless that is your choice. Greener living can be compatible with modern living through a process of reconciliation, discovery and integration: reconciliation of your ideals, discovery of replacements and integration of those replacements into your life. You'll soon realize that what you're losing is an advantage and a relief, and what you're gaining is infinitely more satisfying: a healthier, simpler, more balanced life that will have the Joneses envying you.

SUPPORTING ENVIRONMENTAL CAUSES MEANS GIVING UP TIME I DON'T HAVE (E.G., VOLUNTEERING AND WRITING LOTS OF LETTERS).

Today's busy student, professional or caregiver doesn't need to lead campaigns and construct manifestos to have their opinions counted. The Internet has made it easier than ever to acquire timely information on actionable issues and send pre-written letters of support or protest that target decision makers.

Organizations working on a range of issues from environmental protection to corporate and government accountability are enabling people to take action from the privacy of their home or office with very little time spent. Anyone with access to a computer and the Internet can sign petitions and send letters to decision makers just by going online. It's never been simpler to participate in influencing environmental policy. *Chapter 6: Getting Involved* discusses this subject at some length.

IT'S HYPOCRITICAL TO ADVOCATE AND PRACTICE ENVIRONMENTALLY FRIENDLY BEHAVIORS IN SOME, BUT NOT ALL, AREAS OF MY LIFE.

Greener living is a relative and evolving state. Being somewhere between the beginning and the middle (there really is no "end") of a journey entailing discovery, evaluation and adaptation automatically means that there will always be questions, more to do and things you could do better.

Hypocrisy comes into play only if you give false information about your attributes or demand a standard from another that you won't live up to yourself. If you scold your neighbor for wasting water in their yard, you best be practicing water conservation on your side of the fence. But possessing the desire and intention to live greener, while having made only marginal progress to date, doesn't make you a hypocrite, it makes you imperfect. And aren't we all?

Be patient with yourself and your critics who would prefer you abandon your goals to make themselves feel better. Learning to live greener is a process that takes time, and you shouldn't have unrealistic expectations that could sabotage your drive and eventual success. What you're able to achieve is a factor of understanding, timing, location, obligations, finances, and so many other things, so adopt a willingness to be a work in progress—it's really the only way to learn and improve.

NOTHING I DO WILL MAKE A DIFFERENCE IF NO ONE ELSE IS DOING ANYTHING.

No one is alone in their concern for the environment and their conscience to act more thoughtfully to protect its well-being. Your efforts to walk lighter on this earth, support green capitalism and appeal for better environmental policy make a difference, because every act, when multiplied over many days and many people, produces positive results. Remember, even if those changes can't be seen, they are still occurring.

So many people making efforts, large and small, to green their lives adds up to big results for the environmental movement, not only for the cumulative impact of numerous individual actions, but also for the power that one person's example has to bring about positive changes in others. Every day people all over the world exhibit ecological behaviors that raise consciousness and elicit duplication from others who witness them. Change yourself and you will unwittingly change another.

CHAPTER 2:
MAKING A DIFFERENCE

Within the domains of daily living, purchasing and taking action lie our opportunities and our obligations to effect positive change in the world. Every day in this country more than 290 million people go about their lives—lives that in some way impact the natural environment for better or worse. Understanding the relationship between what we do and the larger environment is vital to developing and strengthening a sense of responsibility for the cause and effect of our actions. With new knowledge and a new appreciation for our role in the solution, we can begin to implement meaningful changes.

"The penalty good people pay for not being interested in politics is to be governed by people worse than themselves." **Plato**

EMPOWERING BUSY PEOPLE

The Internet has spawned a new and liberating form of activism referred to as "electronic activism." Electronic activism is convenient, fast and ideal for busy people who want to influence public or corporate policy on their coffee break. The mechanisms of this modern form of activism include action alerts (bulletins explaining the need for public support or protest of a particular deed); a menu of actions to choose from (popular choices include signing a pre-written petition or letter); and finally, the delivery of a communication to an intended audience (via e-mail, fax or U.S. mail).

From getting environmental news to sending letters to Washington, D.C., and CEOs, awareness and activism are being facilitated by the Internet. Organizations like Natural Resource Defense Council, World Wildlife Fund, Sierra Club, and no less than 100 others offer news bulletins to e-mail subscribers and provide opportunities to take a prescribed action in as little as five minutes. It's now quick and easy to learn and respond when the environment's well-being is threatened. Learn more about the efficiency and simplicity of taking action via the Internet in *Chapter 6: Getting Involved.*

GET OUT AND VOTE

Voting, an American right and duty, is not regarded as activism, although it can achieve similar results. Voting gives us a voice in who will form policy that affects our lives and environment, yet in the last presidential election, only 60 percent of eligible voters turned out to participate.

To the chagrin of many, voting can mean choosing between two or more unappealing candidates—vote anyway. Voting asserts that you are an active constituent, meaning your comments and opinions will be given more weight by delegates should you write to them during their term. Also, even if your vote is for the "lesser of two evils," you're still providing a valuable civic service by trying to deny the most dreadful candidate a seat in office!

When it comes to evaluating candidates running for public office, accurate information is critically important. Unfortunately, politicians and popular media (including television and radio) churn out mud-slinging ads, air misleading sound bites, report half truths and innuendoes, and present oversimplified arguments. Yet, not enough people recognize the diminished integrity of the media. According to a study conducted by the Center for Survey Research and Analysis at the University of Connecticut for the Radio and Television News Directors Foundation, most Americans continue to rely

☐☐☐

Turn off the water while brushing your teeth or shaving. Running the water continuously for just two minutes can waste three gallons of water! Fill a cup with water when brushing your teeth and fill the sink bowl to rinse your razor instead of running the water.

☐☐☐

Install water-saving devices in the bathroom if your fixtures are nonconserving. Faucet aerators and low-flow regulators for showerheads can reduce water output by 40 and 50 percent, respectively, while still delivering a satisfactory spray.

☐☐☐

Avoid using your toilet as a wastebasket. Keep a trash can in the bathroom, but if you forget and toss garbage in the toilet bowl, leave it—it will eventually get flushed with normal use.

☐☐☐

Buy a shower curtain that will far outlast cheap plastic ones; a shower curtain made of hemp will naturally resist mildew and is machine washable. (See resources under *Department Stores* in chapter 5.)

☐☐☐

Use a strainer on all drains to catch hair and prevent drain clogs. If you do get a clog, use a metal snake to work the clog loose (available at hardware stores for around $12), not toxic drain cleaners.

Even though it is preferable to use a durable, mildew-resistant hemp shower curtain in place of a vinyl one, many still rely on vinyl. You can take the following steps to get the longest life out of a vinyl curtain:

- Stretch the curtain closed completely after a shower to eliminate folds where moisture cannot easily evaporate.
- Open the bathroom door and a window, if possible, after exiting the shower to allow steam to dissipate.
- Run the exhaust fan for five minutes following a shower.

Fix slow drains. Pour half a cup of baking soda down the drain and follow it with half a cup of white vinegar. Let it sit for twenty minutes to a half hour, then pour boiling water down the drain (about two quarts).

Turn your soap-bar scraps into usable shavings. Using a cheese grater, grate several scraps into shavings and put them in a decorative bowl next to the sink. Just take a pinch from the bowl with a dry hand, add water and work into a lather.

BUILDING AND HOME IMPROVEMENT

If you are planning to build a new home, think smaller. Smaller homes are more efficient and because they have to be planned more creatively to account for traffic patterns, space and storage, they can be much more architecturally interesting than larger structures.

ENERGY

Keep your refrigerator full. Food retains cold better than air does, so a near-empty fridge is working much harder to cool its contents. Don't overstuff your fridge either. Air circulation is needed to cool and control humidity.

Your refrigerator should be set close to 37 degrees Fahrenheit and your freezer set to 3 degrees Fahrenheit to conserve energy. Place a weather thermometer inside the compartment to check its temperature and adjust the dials until you achieve the desired temperature.

Clean refrigerator gaskets regularly and vacuum the condenser coils twice a year. Your refrigerator will operate more efficiently and use less electricity.

Wrap your water heater in an insulating jacket if it is located in an unheated space such as a basement or garage.

Use your microwave. Cooking and reheating with a microwave is faster and more efficient than using the stovetop or oven, thus reducing up to 70 percent of energy use.

Use a toaster oven for small jobs. It will use a third to half as much energy as a full-size oven.

Turn off the oven ten to fifteen minutes before cooking time runs out; food will continue to cook without using the extra electricity.

If you own a dishwasher with a booster heater, make sure it is turned on. Using the booster heater heats the water at the source, so you can set your hot-water tank to a lower temperature (about 120 degrees Fahrenheit). If you're unsure if your model has one, contact the manufacturer.

If you have a "no-heat" dry setting on your dishwasher, use it. Heat drying is not necessary after a hot-wash cycle. If you don't have an air-dry setting on your model, turn the dishwasher off after the final rinse and prop the door open, allowing your dishes to air-dry.

Shift appliance use to off-peak hours. Off-peak hours are typically from 9 p.m. to 7 a.m. Your utility company may also offer off-peak energy rates, in which case you can save money by running appliances during lower-rate periods. Call your utility company to find out if they offer off-peak rates and during what times.

☐☐☐

Arrange furniture to take advantage of natural light from windows. Place desks and reading chairs next to windows to cut down on the need and use of supplemental, artificial light during the day.

☐☐☐

Install dimmer switches where dimmed lighting makes sense, like the dining room and hallways. Dimming a light by 25 percent saves an equal percentage of energy.

☐☐☐

Switch to fluorescent bulbs in areas where extended lighting is required. Though the initial price is higher than for incandescent bulbs, fluorescent lights produce four times as much light per watt, last up to ten times as long and therefore cost one-third as much to operate.

☐☐☐

Reduce the number of bulbs in linear light fixtures that give off more light than you need. Or replace some bulbs with lower-watt bulbs to conserve energy.

☐☐☐

Paint interior walls a light color to reflect light. If you decorate with dark walls, at night, use task lighting to avoid using too many peripheral lights.

Turn off all lights when not in use. If you're worried about running into obstacles while feeling for light switches, invest in some fluorescent night-lights to illuminate halls and rooms just enough to locate switches safely.

Install a motion sensor on lights in stairwells or on dark landings where light is needed only when passing through.

Turn off exterior lights in the morning. Better yet, use a timer or install motion detectors so the lights will only come on when they are needed.

Use an outdoor compact fluorescent light (CFL) that is between 9 and 18 watts if you are lighting outdoor areas for security. A CFL, which does not shine as bright as an incandescent flood spot, will save energy and actually permit better visibility into dark areas that aren't illuminated than brighter floods permit.

Schedule an energy audit to learn more about your energy consumption and what steps you can take to cut energy costs. Many utility companies and service providers perform energy audits at no or low cost to you.

☐☐☐

Install ceiling fans to save money on cooling and heating and reduce energy waste. In the summer, use them in place of a central air conditioner. In the winter, a ceiling fan with a motor that runs in reverse can push warm air down from the ceiling and thus conserve energy.

☐☐☐

Run heat-producing appliances such as washers, dryers, dishwashers and ovens during the cooler hours of the day in the summer months.

☐☐☐

Don't place lamps with incandescent bulbs near your air-conditioning thermostat. The heat given off by them will register on the thermostat, causing the air conditioner to run longer than necessary.

☐☐☐

Set central air-conditioning units as high as is comfortable. For each degree above 78, you'll save 6 to 8 percent in cooling costs.

☐☐☐

Keep windows and drapes closed on hot days to reduce radiant solar gain.

☐☐☐

If you are heating an outdoor pool, cover your pool at night to conserve 40 to 70 percent of energy that would otherwise go up in steam.

"That which we persist in doing becomes easier for us to do; not that the nature of the thing itself is changed, but that our power to do is increased."
Ralph Waldo Emerson

Check air conditioner filters; they should be cleaned or replaced monthly to help the unit run at peak efficiency. If you have an outdoor unit, make sure its coils are unobstructed by debris, plants or shrubs.

In hot climates, block or filter direct sunlight into your home by shading windows on the south and west sides of the house with awnings, trees or shrubs.

Set your thermostat no higher than 68 degrees in winter. This is a very comfortable temperature if you are dressed properly.

Take extra steps to maximize heating efficiency when the weather turns cold.
- Close shades and curtains to reduce heat loss as soon as the sun goes down.
- Open all the shades and curtains during the day, except those on north-facing windows, to take advantage of solar heat gain.
- Close doors and vents to rooms that are not being used.

Install a thermostat that can be programmed to turn down the heat at bedtime, and turn it back up just before you wake in the morning. This could save you up to 20 percent on heating costs.

Make sure your furnace is working at peak efficiency. One simple thing you can do is clean or replace the filter monthly or as needed.

Apply door sweeps to the bottom of exterior doors and install weather stripping to minimize gaps and thus heat loss.

When shopping for new appliances, look for those equipped with energy-efficient standby power devices that use one watt or less of energy per hour. Without these devices, appliances can draw four to seven watts per hour even when unused, and the Department of Energy estimates that approximately twenty-six power plants are needed just to power these so-called "energy vampires."

Change the setting of the power-saving feature on your computer so that during periods of inactivity, your computer shuts down the monitor at five minutes, the hard drive at thirty minutes, and finally puts the computer in sleep mode at thirty-five minutes.

Purchase Tradable Renewable Energy Certificates (TRCs) or "green tags." More renewable electricity is generated and delivered into the regional power pool, thus displacing an equal amount of other conventional electricity generation, such as coal, oil, and large hydro or natural gas. To learn more, see resources under *Energy* in chapter 7.

Learn how to make an efficient and clean fire in your fireplace by following these steps:
1. Loosely crumple newspaper (uncolored) on the floor of the firebox. Use less if your kindling is fine and dry, more if the opposite is the case.
2. Place finely split, dry kindling on top of and behind the paper. Top it off with two to three small pieces of firewood.
3. Open all air controls and light the newspaper in several places to achieve rapid ignition. Then, quickly close the "front door" halfway to create a strong draft. In seconds, you'll have a bright, hot fire.
4. To this, add several small pieces of firewood, being careful not to smother the fire.

Note: These suggestions are general guidelines and apply to many wood-burning systems. However, consult your operation manual for special firing techniques that may be required for your system.

Use an electric, propane or natural gas grill instead of burning charcoal or wood briquettes, which produce harmful smoke when burned. *Note:* If your electricity comes from coal-burning power plants, avoid an electric grill.

HAZARDOUS WASTE

Become familiar with what common household items contain potentially hazardous ingredients, and then take steps to find nonhazardous alternatives. For a list of common household products with potentially hazardous ingredients, see resources under *Green Cleaning* in chapter 7.

Use a small garbage can in your garage to dispose of hazardous waste in their original containers. When it becomes full, take it to a hazardous waste treatment center.

Dispose of expired medicines by calling your pharmacy or local hospital to find out if they have a collection stand from which a company picks up expired medicine and sees to its safe disposal or destruction. If neither do, contact your local hazardous waste disposal center for instructions.

HOLIDAYS

Limit the number of gifts you buy for people. Pick a single family member's name out of a hat and give a gift only to that person. Also, suggest a gift theme of earth-friendly gifts that won't harm the environment.

Choose gifts that support reuse. Visit local antiques shops where you can find some real treasures that are bargains too.

Give gifts that don't come with a lot of packaging or require wrapping. Examples include event tickets, gift certificates, money and memberships.

Give the ultimate nonmaterial gift for Christmas this year—your time and/or talent. Examples include:

- Baby-sitting or pet-sitting
- Granting a special favor
- Teaching another a skill you have which they have always admired and wanted to learn
- A date including tickets to a special event or performance

Give your holiday a different meaning and focus: start traditions that don't center around gift giving, like annual game tournaments, cook-offs, book discussions, craft sessions, etc. These activities can still center around family and a traditional feast, while providing more joy and fulfillment than a material gift.

Buy gift wrap made from recycled paper. If your store does not sell recycled gift wrap, ask them to please stock it in the future. (See resources under *Paper Products* in chapter 5.)

Save used wrapping paper for next year. Save boxes that collapse, bows, ribbons and gift bags too. When it's time to recycle wrapping paper, make sure the paper is recyclable. If you're not sure, check with your local recycling company for guidelines.

Instead of buying wrapping paper to wrap gifts, use materials from around the house that can serve as gift wrap. Root out and use any of the following for earth-friendly wrapping:
- Old posters and maps
- Old sheet music
- Wallpaper scraps
- Scarves and pillowcases
- Fabric remnants
- Colorful ads or photos torn out of magazines and catalogs

Minimize wrapping this year by choosing an alternative way to present your gifts. Here are some ideas:
- Many of the paper carrying bags you get from stores during the holiday shopping season are festive enough to double as gift bags.
- If you purchase an item that comes in a large box, place it under the tree on Christmas Eve and drape a scarf or throw blanket over it.
- Clothing items can be rolled and tied in the middle with a wide silk ribbon.
- Small items, such as a necklace, can be stuck deep in the Christmas tree. On Christmas morning, make the recipient search among the branches for their gift.
- Items for the house can be placed where they will eventually be kept and used with just a bow and card attached. Throughout the day, the recipient will discover their gifts.

Buy a permanent tree instead of a disposable one. An artificial tree will last a lifetime.

Recycle your Christmas tree within the first week after December 25th, so you don't miss the chance. Mulching, chipping or composting Christmas trees after the holidays is an earth-wise alternative to throwing them into landfills. In many counties, for a limited time following Christmas, trees will be picked up for recycling if left at the curb. Call your recycling company for details. Remove all trimmings before taking the tree from your home. If your community doesn't provide Christmas tree recycling services, visit *gardenweb.com* for ideas on how to use your discarded tree at home.

Buy a living Christmas tree to transplant in your yard. This can be a good option for anyone with the desire, space and climate to transplant live trees in January. A live tree should remain inside for no longer than three to five days, and placed in a cool room that is free of hot or cold drafts. Transplanting a tree in December/January is risky, so consult a local nursery before choosing a live tree.

Use less energy for holiday lights by following these tips:
- Choose strings with fewer bulbs and the fewest watts per bulb.
- Choose LED lights, which are more energy efficient than incandescent ones.
- Operate your lights for no more than four hours a night and use a programmable timer so they will not accidentally remain on overnight.

Note: LED lights may be hard to find locally. To purchase online, visit *ledup.com, realgoods.com* or *giftsfourseasons.com/ledlighting.html.*

Make your own gift tags out of last year's Christmas cards by cutting out the design on the card.

Send the fronts of holiday greeting cards you receive to St. Jude's Ranch for Children. The children in St. Jude's care make and sell new cards from the old ones they receive. Mail card fronts to *St. Jude's Ranch for Children, 100 St. Jude's Street, P.O. Box 60100, Boulder City, Nevada, 89006.*

KITCHEN/MEALS

Buy organic foods. Organic farms use natural growing practices that promote sustainable agriculture and provide healthy alternatives to conventional crops grown with pesticides and genetically modified organisms. Ask your grocer's produce manager to stock organic produce.

Seek out local farmers' markets and buy locally grown, seasonal produce to cut down on environmental costs associated with transporting produce to your community from great distances. (See resources under *Safe Food and Sustainable Agriculture* in chapter 7.)

Eat less meat. Reducing your meat consumption would reduce food-related land use and water pollution problems.

Purchase a water-filtration system if you're concerned about your drinking water, instead of relying on bottled water.

Buy fish that are not caught or farmed in ways that harm the environment. (See resources under *Safe Food and Sustainable Agriculture* in chapter 7.)

Reuse glass jars for food storage. Plastic food tubs, such as those used for yogurt, can also be reused. (See guidelines for reusing plastic in this chapter under *Reduce/Reuse/Recycle*.) For larger portions of leftovers, use soup and mixing bowls, then fit the top with a saucer or plate in place of plastic wrap.

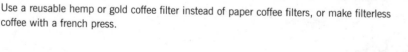

Buy several cloth napkins and use them instead of paper at home and on the go. Cloth napkins can be used several times before washing. Give each family member a unique napkin ring to store their napkin between meals.

Use a reusable hemp or gold coffee filter instead of paper coffee filters, or make filterless coffee with a french press.

When ordering takeout, take steps to reduce the waste it will produce. If you're taking it home, don't take what you won't need (e.g., napkins, flatware, etc.). If the food is being delivered, ask your order-taker to write "NO NAPKINS, FLATWARE OR CONDIMENTS" directly on the order ticket.

☐☐☐

Fill a bowl with cold water and wash fruit and vegetables this way, instead of letting water from a faucet run over them.

☐☐☐

Make sure the kitchen faucet is in the "cold" position when turning it on for brief periods. You'll waste significant energy turning on the hot water even before hot water starts to flow.

☐☐☐

Install a tankless, instant water heater inside the cabinet under your kitchen sink if your hot-water tank is located some distance from your kitchen, and you typically have to run the water a long time before it turns hot. This will save considerable water and energy.

☐☐☐

Store a pitcher or bottle with water in the refrigerator instead of running the kitchen faucet until the water runs cold enough for you to drink.

☐☐☐

Turn the faucet on at a fraction of full volume for things like washing hands and rinsing dishes to save considerable water.

☐☐☐

Cut back on or stop using single-serving and single-use products that consume needless extra paper and plastic for packaging.

"The reward of a thing well done is to have done it."
Ralph Waldo Emerson

Reuse water leftover after common household uses to water plants instead of pouring it down the drain (e.g., from a double boiler, washing produce, steaming vegetables, cooking pasta, soaking beans, soaking frozen meat in its packaging, etc.). Transfer leftover water to a watering can for later use. Make sure water is cool before using it to water plants.

Buy in bulk whenever possible, thus avoiding the excess packaging that comes from buying smaller quantities.

Cook in bulk when you can to store away future lunches in reusable containers. Packing leftovers to work or school means you can avoid takeout and all its packaging.

Use the dishwasher only for full loads for the most efficient water use. If you have a small number of dishes or pans to clean, wash them by hand. You'll save the most water by filling a basin with just three to four inches of water, stacking the dishes as you wash them, and then rinsing them quickly under a light stream of water.

If your dishwasher can handle it, scrape but don't rinse dishes before putting them in the dishwasher. If dishes do have to be rinsed first, try to rinse them immediately after preparing food or eating—before food has had a chance to harden.

Use an electric or chimney briquette starter on charcoal, not lighter fluid, to reduce the toxins emitted from outdoor cookouts.

Choose human-powered lawn and garden equipment if you can get the job done without gas-fueled equipment. For larger jobs, electric equipment may also be substituted. (See resources under *Outdoors/Lawn and Garden* in chapter 5.)

Compost your leaves and yard trimmings and divert compostable material from overburdened landfills. If you don't have room to compost on your property, take yard waste to a local yard debris recycler. Call your local transfer station or dump to inquire.

Protect land you own from unwanted development. Join a land trust and create a conservation easement to ensure permanent protection for specified land. There are over 1,400 local and regional land trusts across the country. To find one, see resources under *Livable Communities* in chapter 7.

REDUCE/REUSE/RECYCLE

Buy products of quality that will last a long time. Avoid buying products that are made cheaply, to be used once and then disposed.

Buy rechargeable batteries and a battery charger. Most rechargeable batteries can be recharged up to 1,000 times.

Replace alkaline batteries in portable devices with rechargeable NiCd, NiMH or Lithium-ion batteries. Check with the manufacturer on compatibility.

Recycle rechargeable batteries that no longer hold a charge. Find the nearest battery drop-off location by going to **rbrc.org** online or by calling *1-800-8-BATTERY.*

Discharge rechargeable NiCd or NiMH batteries completely before recharging. Recharging these types of batteries when only partially depleted can damage them, leading to more frequent replacement. Go to **greenbatteries.com** to learn about the different types of rechargeable batteries and to purchase batteries and chargers.

Take worn-out rechargeable battery packs for cordless tools and appliances to a merchant that can rebuild the battery. To find such a merchant, look under "Batteries" in the phone book.

☐☐☐

Upgrade old computers with new memory, microprocessors and drives. Or donate them to a computer refurbisher or recycler. Do not let them end up in a landfill where their toxic materials can pose environmental hazards. To locate recycling and reuse organizations, see resources under *Reduce, Reuse and Recycle* in chapter 7.

☐☐☐

Never throw a cell phone into the trash—see that it gets reused or recycled. Cell phones have a toxic waste stream including lead, mercury and cadmium. When discarded improperly, these toxins are released into the environment. To find out how to recycle your unwanted cell phone, see resources under *Reduce, Reuse and Recycle* in chapter 7.

☐☐☐

Buy a paper shredder and use it to shred nonrecyclable paper. Then use the shredded paper as packing material.

☐☐☐

Cut worn-out clothes, bedding and towels into squares and use the pieces as cleaning rags, handkerchiefs or napkins.

☐☐☐

Use old and worn-out clothing, sheets, bedspreads and drapes for sewing projects. If you're not crafty or haven't the need, donate clean items to a sewing or quilting group.

THE IMPORTANCE OF BEING BETTER INFORMED

The environment—complicated, misunderstood and recondite—suffers when the masses fail to understand how to reduce their ecological footprint. Decisions based on a lack of knowledge or misinformation can and do lead to errors in judgment, or simply oversights, with unintentional consequences. And oftentimes people act hastily or negligently when they know better, but do so because solutions elude them precisely when they are needed. Information is invaluable to forming decisions and making choices that can better protect our world, but we can't be experts on everything—and we don't need to be. Taking advantage of what the Internet has to offer, an able and willing individual can access information on just about any subject.

A click of the mouse can now put information before you that previously was only attainable through industrious searches through libraries of one sort or another or by special request. Access to timely and extensive information and viewpoints via the Internet not only leads to a more informed citizenry, but it is also requisite for revolutionizing our thoughts and living habits, since daily choices and habits are an outgrowth of what we know and believe. A pursuit of knowledge that can impart wisdom and reveal solutions is essential to making intelligent, deliberate and purposeful decisions in our lives.

INFORMATION THE BUSY PERSON CAN USE

Granted, the Internet is a vast oasis of information, but it is also a free-for-all—a conglomeration of sites of credible and dubious origin and purpose, the merited and the inappropriate, the intelligent as well as the inane, and the verbose versus the laconic. With so much to sort through, the trick to getting quick, applicable results from the Internet may be to have someone else do the sorting. And on certain matters of environmental importance, this book has done just that.

The only satisfactory end result to using the Web sites selected below, is that busy people can trust and make use of what is provided to become a smarter, more productive and effectual steward of the environment. For a Web site, or specific Web page as the case may be, to be deemed suitable, it had to satisfy the following criteria:

- It covers a subject of either popular or critical importance.
- The content is concise and to the point.
- The presentation and explanation are clear and straightforward.
- The source is credible and reliable.

Not all resources will perfectly meet these criteria in the eyes of the discriminating reader; nonetheless, the resources herein

"If anyone can show me, and prove to me, that I am wrong in thought or deed, I will gladly change. I seek the truth, which never yet hurt anybody. It is only persistence in self-delusion and ignorance which does harm."
Marcus Aurelius

provide excellent information that can prepare you to make better decisions for yourself and the environment.

Some of the Web page addresses, or URLs (URL stands for Uniform Resource Locator), provided below are longer than you may be used to seeing. These longer URLs circumvent the site's home page, taking you instantly deeper into its directories and substantive content. Bypassing a Web site's home page can save the busy person a lot of time, but there can be a down side: due to the dynamic and constantly changing nature of the Web, site administrators sometimes modify URLs faster than any printed index can keep up with them. You have a few options if you type one of the URLs provided below into your Internet browser's window and are served an error message:

1. Revert to the Web site's home page address (the home page address is comprised of all characters preceding the first forward slash), and navigate the site until you find a link to the referenced information.
2. From the Web site's home page, locate the "Contact Us" or "E-mail" link, and send a request for the updated URL and wait for a reply.

> **To link to these Web pages, visit this book's companion Web site at *greenmatters.com* and click on "Helpful Links."**

Of course, other good resources on the following, and other, subjects can be found online. When surfing the Internet, use a search engine that ranks high in terms of delivering accurate results. Google has earned consistently high marks for relevant searches, overall usability and comprehensive results. You can find the latest reviews of Internet search engines at Search Engine Watch (*searchenginewatch.com*) or Search Engine Showdown (*searchengineshowdown.com*). Once you select a search engine, navigate that site for its search tips. Every engine is a little different, and knowing how to use a particular one will refine your search results, increasing what you can achieve online in less time.

BUILDING AND HOME IMPROVEMENT
Whether building a new home or remodeling an existing one, every decision you make has consequences to the environment. In new home construction, your choice for site location, home size, design, and material and product specification will determine your home's impact on the environment now and for years to come. When remodeling, responsible dismantling and disposal are just as important as planning for the addition or renovation. Generally, a home should not exceed what you need and

construction and design should include the application of nontoxic, renewable and low-impact materials and technologies to the fullest extent possible.

buildinggreen.com
Informative articles and a comprehensive directory of green building products are available to Web site subscribers, or buy a hard copy of the GreenSpec directory, with over 1,400 product descriptions, environmental characteristics and considerations, and manufacturer contact information.

greenhomebuilding.com
Provides a good introduction to different sustainable building considerations with links to books and an "Expert Advice" Q&A forum.

greenbuilder.com/sourcebook
Information on green building systems and materials including definitions, considerations, market status, implementation issues and guidelines.

oikos.com/products
Search by product type to find manufacturers of sustainable building materials and finishes.

usgbc.org
Locate a builder accredited by the U.S. Green Building Council under their Leadership in Energy and Environmental Design Program (LEED).

salvageweb.com
build.recycle.net
If your city is short on businesses that cater to those wanting to take advantage of architectural salvage and used building materials, try searching one of these online materials exchanges.

rehabadvisor.pathnet.org
Guidelines for conducting an energy-efficient house renovation.

eartheasy.com/live_nontoxic_paints.htm
Find an excellent article on how to choose safer paint coatings.

organicarchitect.com/pdf/countertops.pdf
This article will help the kitchen remodeler sort out the eco-benefits, the eco-impacts and the relative costs of several countertop materials.

CORPORATE ACCOUNTABILITY AND CONSUMER PROTECTION

Corporations' profit-driven interests often overpower consideration for the well-being of natural resources, the environment and public health. With the help of watchdog organizations that specialize in investigating and reporting on criminal or deleterious acts by corporations, you'll know when and why to pull your support of a company.

corpwatch.org
Information on corporate improprieties every consumer should know about.

prwatch.org
Get the facts behind misleading public relations campaigns designed to trick consumers and voters.

responsibleshopper.org
Before you buy, learn more about the companies behind the products. A searchable database allows the user to find reports on over 350 different companies.

eco-labels.org
The Consumers Union's searchable database of eco-labels allows users to review an independent evaluation of several labels used on food, personal hygiene, household cleaners, and wood and paper products.

chemicalindustryarchives.org
The real and present danger of many widely used chemicals has motivated chemical manufacturers to spend a great deal of money to "convince" the public that we have nothing to worry about, but we do, as documents at this Web site attest.

ENERGY

Nationally, our reliance primarily on fossil fuels for electricity has taken a sizeable toll on the environment. The burning of fossil fuels such as coal, gas and oil is the leading man-made cause of ozone depleting CO_2 and the second leading cause of smog-forming nitrogen oxide. And massive hydro-power dams have forever altered the natural flow of rivers and devastated native fish populations by inhibiting their migration. Conserving energy at home and work, and switching to renewable, clean energy sources will help to diminish the need for, and the effects of, dirty and nature-altering sources of power.

www.eere.energy.gov
www.nrel.gov
www.repp.org
These energy information sites provide information on renewable-energy technologies, energy facts and figures, and resources for further learning.

energystar.gov/products
Make energy-efficient choices when buying appliances, electronics, lighting, etc. Energy Star, a project of the U.S. EPA, tests and qualifies energy-efficient products in thirty-eight product categories. Identify Energy Star–rated products and locate stores through their Web site.

"The end of the human race will be that it will eventually die of civilization."
Ralph Waldo Emerson

GLOBAL WARMING

The rapid climate change, by historical measures, which the earth has experienced in the last 120 years, is primarily due to human activities like burning fossil fuels. Escalating concentrations of greenhouse gases resulting from the combustion of fossil fuels has the effect of trapping heat in the earth's atmosphere. As the earth warms out of step with its natural cycle, glaciers are melting, arctic ice is thinning, ocean levels are rising and coral reefs are dying from overheated waters.

*www.ncdc.noaa.gov/oa/climate/
globalwarming.html*
A scientific yet understandable explanation of global warming.

climate.org
Overview of critical topics related to global warming with links to more resources on each topic.

GREEN CLEANING

During their use, cleaning products can be harmful by way of contact, inhalation or ingestion. And most of the cleaners and solvents used in and outside the home will end up in the environment via storm drains or sewers. If dangerous chemicals are present, vegetation, wildlife and water quality can be affected. Transitioning to green cleaning can be as easy as opening your pantry. Baking soda, vinegar, salt,

lemon juice and olive oil are just some of the ingredients that can be combined to safely and effectively clean your home from top to bottom.

*epa.gov/grtlakes/seahome/housewaste/house/
products.htm*
A glossary of common household products, their hazardous constituents and risks of exposure.

es.epa.gov/techinfo/facts/safe-fs.html
Fast facts on household cleaners, a list of toxic ingredients to avoid, alternatives to commercial products you can whip up yourself and resources for more information.

cnt.org/wetcleaning/final-report/learned
Find out more about professional wet cleaning—a safer alternative to dry cleaning.

nybg.org/plants/factsheets/cleanair.html
Houseplants that can improve indoor air quality.

LIVABLE COMMUNITIES

Sprawl has increased automobile dependence, seen vast tracts of open space and farmland paved over, isolated suburbanites from vibrant community centers, and brought industrial zones and residential communities closer to each other. The adverse impacts to wildlife, air, water and our quality of life has incited several organizations to design and promote anti-sprawl packages to help citizens organize and combat thoughtless development.

As for the not-so-visible assaults on our communities, Internet databases are helping citizens identify polluters by zip code. Once polluters have been identified, you can share your findings and concerns with community leaders and local or state environmental advocacy groups to induce corrective action.

empowermentinstitute.net/files/LNP.html
The Livable Neighborhood Program promotes initiatives designed to work at the neighborhood level to improve the overall livability of communities.

sierraclub.org/sprawl
The Sierra Club identifies both the problems and solutions of sprawl and directs the reader to resources for further reading in their comprehensive online guide to stopping sprawl.

ceds.org
Download Community & Environmental Defense Services' free publication, "Preserving Neighborhoods & the Environment from Unsustainable Land Development Projects: A Citizen's Guide to Forming a Winning Strategy"—a guide to 150 actions found to be most effective in identifying and preventing the impacts of development projects.

bikewalk.org
This site can help you create neighborhoods and communities where people walk and bicycle.

lta.org/conserve/index.html
nature.org/joinanddonate/giftandlegacy
Protect your undeveloped land from the threat of development. Land Trust Alliance and The Nature Conservancy explain options that are open to landowners who want their land protected now or for the future.

darksky.org
Learn how to fight light pollution in your community.

scorecard.org
rtk.net
How insulated is your community from polluters? Retrieve available information on local pollution and who's responsible from these online databases.

communitygreens.org
pps.org
Resources, case studies, and publications to help citizens create or preserve parks and public spaces that build and nurture communities.

cohousing.org
Find out more about eco/community living options that can conserve land and foster community.

MEDIA

The increasingly corporate-controlled media is arguably limiting the viewpoints we have access to. In broadcast news in particular, there is evidence of misdirected journalistic priorities, obvious political biases, a compulsion to sensationalize events and spinning news stories to influence public opinion. A certain amount of frustration and skepticism on the part of viewers is justified, but don't stew or settle—seek out the truth and find alternatives to mainstream news broadcasts and publications.

fair.org
Fairness and Accuracy in Reporting, by exposing well-documented examples of media bias and censorship, is making it a little easier for news watchers to know who to trust for honest and diverse reporting. Access the latest edition of their weekly radio program CounterSpin, for news that mainstream media isn't reporting.

prwatch.org/spin
The Center for Media and Democracy's daily bulletin entitled Spin of the Day reports on spin and propaganda in the media from the previous news day.

altpress.org
alternet.org
mediachannel.org
npr.org
Use these resources for better access to independent and alternative journalism.

OFFICE/BUSINESS

Waste management and energy use are increasing concerns for businesses—and an opportunity to lower operating costs and increase profits. Several state and federal programs are working to assist businesses in implementing waste reduction, recycling and energy-wise programs to improve the bottom line while providing relief to the environment.

It's not just what's going on inside office buildings that is cause for increased business participation in solutions that work. Commuting trends have increased transportation-based pollution: the number of people driving to work in a private car has steadily increased since 1985, while the percentage of workers carpooling has declined and transit's share of commuters has changed little. Compounding the effects of increased vehicle use is the increase in distance traveled due to the migration of the American family away from city and business centers.[2] Solutions for commuters can and should encompass employer assistance since several studies show that implementing work options that reduce commuting, such as compressed work weeks and telecommuting, increase employee productivity and retention.[3]

naturalstep.org
Helps visionary companies achieve sustainability and profitability through cost savings and product and service innovation.

> "Human history becomes more and more a race between education and catastrophe." **H. G. Wells**

greenbiz.com
Provides businesses with access to tools and information that can facilitate their transition to more sustainable business practices.

environmentaldefense.org/alliance/officetips. html
A handy guide for office personnel on greening the office.

epa.gov/epaoswer/non-hw/reduce/wstewise
The EPA's WasteWise program helps interested businesses develop, implement and measure waste-reduction activities to eliminate costly municipal solid waste, benefiting the bottom line and the environment.

epa.gov/greenpower/join
Join the EPA's Green Power Partnership and commit to the purchase of green power. Available assistance, tool kits and resources help partners purchase green power and promote their involvement in the program.

safeclimate.net/business/index.php
epa.gov/climateleaders
Information and tools to help businesses of any size begin to manage their greenhouse gas emissions, demonstrate leadership and make a meaningful impact on the climate.

ofee.gov/recycled/cal-index.htm
This easy-to-use paper calculator allows you to compare the environmental impacts of paper with different post-consumer recycled content.

rethinkpaper.org
Determine which tree-free or recycled-content paper best fits your needs with the interactive "Paper Selector."

svtc.org/cleancc/index.html
Silicon Valley Toxics Coalition's annual scorecard of the most environmentally responsible computer companies.

techrecycle.com
interconrecycling.com
recyclingsupersite.com
Business solutions for recycling obsolete computers and eliminating storage and disposal liabilities. See also, *Reduce, Reuse and Recycle* on page 154.

commuterchoice.gov
Enroll your business in the Commuter Choice program and get help adopting solutions that reduce commuter driving.

sustainablebusiness.com/jobs
Whether hiring or looking to be hired, this is one of the most current and comprehensive databases of job openings at sustainable businesses or within the environmental field. If you want to post a résumé, try *greenbiz.com/jobs.*

POPULATION AND THE ENVIRONMENT

By many accounts, the explosive population growth over the past forty years has been the largest contributing factor to environmental degradation. Increased demand for housing, food, water, fuel and nonessential consumables is stressing the earth beyond its capacity to regenerate. If you think the population problem and solution resides with the developing countries that out populate the United States by 3 to 1, think again. The average American consumes over twenty-five times more resources than the average person from a developing country.[4] The World Wildlife Fund's annual Living Planet Report estimates that the human population and resource consumption has surpassed the earth's carrying capacity. If current tendencies in reproduction and consumption do not change, we will experience the complete collapse of critical ecological assets this century.[5]

populationaction.org/issues
worldpopulationbalance.org/pop
Fact sheets and answers to questions about population and natural resources.

plannedparenthood.org/health
Voluntary family-planning resources.

myfootprint.org
Test your ecological footprint.

REDUCE, REUSE AND RECYCLE

Most people associate recycling with admirable environmental stewardship. However, recycling is the third step in a three-step process. Effective waste reduction and resource protection relies on first reducing the amount we consume; second, reusing that which still has a useful life; and third, recycling when something is beyond repair or reuse.

isharestuff.org
This site helps you share specific belongings, e.g., high-cost or seldom-used things, with family and friends. Whether it's your pickup truck or a hot-glue gun, useful things you own, and want your friends to know you'll lend, can be posted here and they'll be notified. Before you know it, people you'll lend to will start their own accounts and post things you can borrow from them.

freecycle.org
craigslist.org
The surest and fastest way to find a second home for acceptable quality items you no longer have a use for is to give them away for free. Post items, or look for things yourself, at one of these Web sites organized by city.

mothering.com/articles/new_baby/diapers/
  joy-of-cloth.html
thediaperhyena.com
Find almost everything you ever wanted or needed to know about cloth diapering.

"If future generations are to remember us with gratitude rather than contempt, we must leave them something more than the miracles of technology. We must leave them a glimpse of the world as it was in the beginning, not just after we got through with it." **Lyndon B. Johnson**

fleamarketguide.com
collectors.org/FM
For used merchandise, get acquainted with flea markets, swap meets and antiques fairs in your region.

obviously.com/recycle
Obvious Implementation Corporation's online recycling guide is full of valuable information on basic recycling, recycling obscure materials and reducing unwanted junk mail.

earth911.org
Provide your zip code upon entering the Web site to locate municipal recycling centers or to find out where to recycle specific items. Don't assume something can't be recycled or donated for reuse until you've checked here first.

wirelessfoundation.org/DonateaPhone
collectivegood.com
wirelessrecycling.com
Donate used wireless phones. They will either be refurbished for a charity in need or recycled in an environmentally sound manner.

greendisk.com
ecodisk.com
Recycling solutions for your personal or business media products and more.

techsoup.org/recycle/10tips.cfm
If you're going to donate an old computer, do it right; follow Compumentor's "Ten Tips for Donating a Computer."

epa.gov/epaoswer/osw/conserve/plugin
The EPA, through its Plug-In To eCycling campaign, is making it easier to recycle electronics by indexing businesses that take back used and obsolete electronics.

ciwmb.ca.gov/RCP
The Recycled Content Product Directory, a project of California's Integrated Waste Management Board is a searchable database of all kinds of recycled products. You can even specify a minimum recycled content for your search results.

SAFE FOOD AND SUSTAINABLE AGRICULTURE
To achieve sustainable agriculture and protect the food supply, our agricultural practices must succeed in protecting area, biodiversity, topsoil, water supply and livestock health. Consumer buying trends will determine what is produced and will drive the policy that regulates agriculture. Therefore, your informed purchases are needed to send the appropriate and intended message to food growers and producers and to the regulatory agencies charged with protecting consumer and agricultural interests alike.

theorganicreport.org
Organic news and articles including "Questions and Answers about Organic" and "Buying Organic: Considering the Real Costs."

factoryfarm.org
GRACE's Family Farm Project defines the factory farm and provides current news and information about factory farm issues by topic (e.g., dairy, poultry, fish, etc.) and region.

gene-watch.org/programs/food/foodFAQ. html
foei.org/gmo/faq.html
Frequently asked questions on GMOs are answered by the Council for Responsible Genetics and Friends of the Earth International.

foe.org/safefood/companylist.html
In the absence of a labeling system for GE foods, Friends of the Earth has compiled a list to help consumers identify companies known to use GE ingredients.

truefoodnow.org/shoppersguide
The True Food Shopping Guide identifies GE-free brands in several categories.

ucsusa.org/food_and_environment/biotech-nology/page.cfm?pageID=337
The Union of Concerned Scientists' guide to GE crops allowed in the U.S. food supply.

renewableenergyworks.com/sustainability/ meatless.html
The environmental consequences of eating meat are summarized in "Eating Green: A Re-examination of Diet in Light of Environmental Concerns," by Walter Simpson. Simpson's article touches on nearly all the major issues including inefficient land use, water scarcity and pollution, loss of biodiversity, depletion of fossil fuels, global warming, deforestation, and native species decline.

veg.ca/living/veg-position-paper.html
Learn more about a vegetarian diet, which can be healthful, nutritionally adequate, and provide health benefits in the prevention and treatment of certain diseases.

localharvest.org
Search for farmers' markets, family farms, food co-ops and restaurants selling locally produced, organic food.

csacenter.org
Community Supported Agriculture (CSA) connects local farms with local consumers, encourages land stewardship, develops a regional food supply and strong local economy, and promotes the economic viability of small, family farms. This site enables visitors to locate CSA farms by state or get help forming a CSA network.

eatwellguide.org
Enter your zip code to find where you can

buy sustainably raised meat, poultry, dairy and eggs near your home.

foodnews.org
A report card of the best and worst produce choices relative to pesticide contamination.

mbayaq.org/cr/seafoodwatch.asp
Monterey Bay Aquarium's Seafood Watch program educates shoppers on the least to most sustainable seafood choices. From their Web site, download a free wallet-size chart to refer to when buying seafood.

farmtoschool.org
Transform your child's school lunch program into one that supports local farmers, sustainability and healthy food choices.

thehia.org/hempfacts.htm
abouthemp.com
If you haven't heard about industrial hemp yet, it's time you knew of its history, vast applications and superior qualities. Refer to chapter 5 to locate hemp products and support the hemp industry.

TRANSPORTATION
It's been said that driving a car is the single most polluting thing the average person does in a day. Biking, walking, ride sharing, consolidating trips and taking public transportation when feasible are alternatives that pay big dividends to the environment. Short of leaving the car at home, adopting better driving habits and driving a low-emissions vehicle can help reduce the impacts from driving.

Automobiles aren't the only mode of transportation relying on expanded infrastructure, emitting greenhouse gases, and consuming scarce and finite petroleum supplies, but because they are the main source of transportation for most Americans, what we drive, how we drive and how often we drive stands to make the biggest reduction in transportation-related environmental impacts.

bts.gov/publications/national_transportation_statistics/
Statistics reveal a conspicuous addiction to cars and very real impacts. If you like numbers, this site has lots: tables on motor vehicle fuel consumption and travel, annual wasted fuel due to congestion, principle means of transportation to work, public road and street mileage, air pollution trends, and over 200 others.

greenercars.com/bestof
The best and worst cars for the environment.

epa.gov/greenvehicles
Look up cars and trucks by vehicle class or a specific model to find scores on air pollution, fuel economy and greenhouse gas emissions.

> "The mystery of a government is not how Washington works, but how to make it stop." **P. J. O'Rourke**

fueleconomy.gov
Find and compare cars side by side on fuel economy, greenhouse gas emissions and air pollution. This site also explains how you can earn a federal income tax deduction if purchasing a "clean-fuel" vehicle before the end of 2006.

suv.org/introductory.html
This site is designed solely to educate consumers on the impacts and dangers of driving an SUV.

fuelcells.org
Vehicles that run on fuel cells are in development and will be available soon. Learn more about the technology and the benefits to the environment.

biodieselamerica.org
biodiesel.org
Information on renewable biodiesel for diesel engines.

runmuki.com/commute
Cycling activist Paul Dorn offers prospective bike commuters tips to make the transition from car to bike easy, safe and fun.

erideshare.com
vanpool.com
Get help connecting with other commuters going your way.

metrocommuterservices.org/costcal.asp
Calculate the cost of driving a car and add it to the many environmental reasons to drive less.

flexcar.com
Joining a car-sharing service can be much cheaper, and lower impact, than owning a vehicle if you rarely need to drive.

TRAVEL AND RECREATION
Travel and tourism is the world's largest industry, and according to the World Tourism Organization, more and more tourists are visiting sensitive natural places. Travelers and recreationists need to be acutely aware of the powerful impact they have on the natural environment. Whether traveling for business or pleasure, plan ahead so you can minimize the potential negative effects from travel.

ecotour.org
Find travel opportunities that benefit local communities and preserve the environment.

greenhotels.com/members.htm
Identify hotels that are committed to reducing waste, conserving resources and reducing or eliminating the use of chemicals.

triplee.com/environment/carbon_offsets.htm
Offset the greenhouse gas emissions produced from your air travel by joining

Better World Club and booking flights through their Travel Cool Program.

oceanconservancy.org/site/DocServer/ fscruiseships.pdf?docID=102
The impacts of cruise ships on the marine environment.

skiareacitizens.com
This environmental scorecard of ski areas grades over seventy western resorts on their environmental policies and practices. For comparison, the National Ski Area Association maintains a database of specific preservation and conservation programs being implemented by ski areas at **nsaa.org/nsaa/environment/the_greenroom**.

lnt.org
When visiting the outdoors, follow the Principles of Leave No Trace to minimize your impact on the natural environment you're passing through.

nrdc.org/water/oceans/ttw/titinx.asp
Natural Resources Defense Council's annual report of water quality at vacation beaches.

VOTING AND POLITICS
Americans have voiced their concern and support for the environment in national polls, yet the recent congressional record is increasingly in favor of loosening public land-use restrictions and environmental regulations. Reversing this trend will require getting better at evaluating candidates running for public office with the help of trustworthy resources, and keeping the pressure on delegates to act in the interest of their constituents while shunning the influences of large donations.

firstgov.org
This is the U.S. government's official information portal. Link to any agency's Web site; find contact information for elected officials at the local, state and federal level; and look up and comment on federal regulations.

lcv.org/scorecard
The League of Conservation Voters' National Environmental Scorecard provides factual information about the environmental voting records of U.S. Representatives and Senators.

vote-smart.org
Project Vote Smart's Web site is comprised of thoroughly-researched data covering candidates and elected officials. This data includes factual information about their voting records, campaign finances, position statements and backgrounds. Project Vote Smart's National Political Awareness Test (NPAT) is a voluntary, comprehensive questionnaire that allows candidates to reveal their issue inclinations to voters. It is a remarkable tool for voters to learn candidates' issue positions and willingness to provide information to the public.

factcheck.org
This organization reveals factual inaccuracies in the statements of politicians, pundits and spokespeople so voters won't be so easily deceived.

citizen.org/litigation/free_info
Public Citizen assists individuals and organizations in accessing information held by government agencies.

gp.org
lp.org
natural-law.org
reformparty.org
constitutionparty.com
Traditional and entrenched thinking from the predominating political parties may not hold the best solutions for today and tomorrow. The advancement of alternative views comes from many sources. Read what other parties are saying about the environment, government spending, taxes, etc. For a complete list of all political parties, visit *politics1.com/parties.htm.*

opensecrets.org
An educational resource on the problem of money in politics.

congress.org/congressorg/megavote
Track your Senators' and Representative's votes by e-mail with MegaVote.

greensheets.com
Analysis of environment, energy and natural resource issues coming before the U.S. Congress.

regulations.gov
Look up federal documents published in the Federal Register open for public comment.

WATER
Population growth has increased water demand for irrigation, domestic use and industry. In heavy-use regions, withdrawals from surface water supplies and groundwater reserves are so high that supplies are being depleted faster than they can be replenished. Serious water shortages in some regions have led to bitter fights over water rights with devastating outcomes for aquatic ecosystems.

On the side of water quality, agricultural and urban runoff, chemical dumping by industries, and careless use and disposal of household hazardous products all contribute to poor water quality in the United States. Much of our water is too dirty for basic uses such as swimming and fishing, and native species are disappearing from our rivers, lakes and coastal waters.

h2ouse.org
Take a virtual tour of a typical home and learn how to reduce water use at home.

epa.gov/owow/nps/whatis.html
Polluted runoff is the leading cause of water quality impairment. From this page on the EPA's Web site, you can learn about key sources of non-point source pollution and what you can do at home and in your community to protect water quality.

epa.gov/epaoswer/non-hw/muncpl/hhw.htm
A list of common household hazardous waste (HHW) products that should always be disposed of at a HHW treatment center.

waterwest.org
Whether you live in the West, consume its agricultural products or just pay federal taxes, every American should be cognizant of what's happening with water in the West.

NOTES

GREEN LIVING MYTHS

1. Steve Hoffman, "Got Organic? Natural Products Expo West Displays Growing Demand for All Things Natural," GreenMoney Journal (Summer 2004).

MAKING A DIFFERENCE

1. Robert B. Jackson and others, "Water in a Changing World," *Issues in Ecology*, no. 9 (Spring 2001): 14.

2. Derek Reiber, "Perfecting Biodegradable Plastics," GreenTide, Tidepool.org (July 2002).

3. Karen Pickett, "Why We Won't Recycle Plastics," *Earth Island Journal 11*, no. 4 (Fall 1996), earthisland.org archives.

4. Rhode Island Resource Recovery Corporation, "Plastic Bags Can Blow You Away!" (brochure).

5. U.S. Environmental Protection Agency, "10 Fast Facts on Recycling," www.epa.gov (accessed September 2005).

6. Reusablebags.com, "Fast Facts," www.reusablebags.com (accessed September 2005).

7. U.S. Environmental Protection Agency, "How We Use Water in These United States," 4.

8. American Water Works Association, www.awwa.org (accessed January 2003).

9. U.S. Department of Transportation, Bureau of Transportation Statistics, "National Transportation Statistics 2004," Tables 1–11 and 1–32.

10. U.S. Department of Energy, Energy Information Administration, "Emissions of Greenhouse Gases in the United States 2003," Chapter 2: Carbon Dioxide Emissions (December 2004): 19–20.

11. U.S. Department of Energy, Energy Information Administration, Petroleum Products Information Sheet, Tables 1.3 and 2.5 (March 2003).

12. Based on 12,000 annual vehicle miles traveled (VMT) and average gas mileage of twenty-four miles per gallon (mpg).

13. American Meat Institute, "Overview of U.S. Meat and Poultry Production and Consumption" (2003): 2.

14. John Robins, *The Food Revolution,* Conari Press (July 11, 2001).

15. The National Public Lands Grazing Campaign, "Troubles with Livestock Grazing," 1, www.publiclandsranching.org (accessed September 2005).

16. United States Senate Committee on Agriculture, Nutrition & Forestry, "Environmental Risks of Livestock & Poultry Production" (1998).

17. U.S. Environmental Protection Agency, 2000 National Water Quality Survey, Sources of Impairment, www.epa.gov.

18. Bureau of Labor Statistics, "Consumer Expenditures in 2003," Report 986, Table A.

19. Temperate Forest Foundation, "Pulp and Paper," *Eco-Link* 8, no. 2: 3.

20. Resource Conservation Alliance, "Using Less Wood Fact Sheet: Focus on Paper Consumption," www.woodconsumption.org (accessed May 2005).

21. Abromovitz & Mattoon, "Paper Cuts: Recovering the Paper Landscape," Worldwatch Institute (1999).

22. Institute of Scrap Recycling Industries, "Recycling Paper" (pamphlet).

23. U.S. Department of Energy, Energy Information Administration, "Emissions of Greenhouse Gases in the United States 2003," Table 6.

24. U.S. Environmental Protection Agency, "Fast Facts: Energy Efficient Lighting," www.epa.gov (accessed May 2005).

25. Based on 2003 EPA mileage estimates; actual fuel efficiency may vary.

26. U.S Department of Energy, Office of Energy Efficiency and Renewable Energy, "Technology Snapshot—Featuring the Toyota Prius," www.fueleconomy.gov (accessed May 2005).

27. Population-Environment Balance, "U.S. Population Growth—Food, Land, Energy, Water, and the U.S. Economy (Fact Sheet)," www.balance.org (accessed September 2005).

ECO-TIPS FOR LIVING GREENER

1. Daily water savings based on saving two quarts per wash, four times a day: (293,655,404 x .02) x (2 x4 ÷ 4) = 11,746,216 gallons. Daily energy savings based on reducing cooking time by one-third using a 15,000 BTU gas cooktop for 40 minutes: (293,655,404 x .01) x (15,000 ÷ 3) = 14,682,770,200 BTUs.

2. U.S. Environmental Protection Agency, Municipal Solid Waste Commodities Fact Sheet: Plastics 2003, www.epa.gov.

BUYING GREEN

1. U.S. Environmental Protection Agency, Office of Pollution Prevention and Toxics, Chemical Hazard Data Availability Study, www.epa.gov (April 2004).

2. Brad Duplisea, "The Real Dope on Beef Hormones," Canadian Health Coalition, www.healthcoalition.ca (accessed September 2005).

GETTING INVOLVED

1. The USFS's decision was immediately challenged by civil liberties, environmental and business groups alike, and the decision is expected to be overturned.

RESOURCES TO HELP THE EARTH

1. Ipsos-Insight Marketing Research, *The Face of the Web 2004.*

2. U.S. Census Bureau, American Housing Survey for the United States, 1985 and 2003 journey to work statistics.

3. Business for Social Responsibility, Issue Brief on Work-Life, bsr.org (accessed May 2005).

4. World Population Balance, www.world-populationbalance.org (accessed May 2005).

5. World Wildlife Fund International, *Living Planet Report 2004.*

INDEX